A Note to Parents

Eyewitness Readers is a compelling new program for beginning readers, designed in conjunction with leading literacy experts, including Dr. Linda Gambrell, President of the National Reading Conference and past board member of the International Reading Association.

Eyewitness has become the most trusted name in illustrated books, and this new series combines the highly visual *Eyewitness* approach with engaging, easy-to-read stories. Each *Eyewitness Reader* is guaranteed to capture a child's interest while developing his or her reading skills, general knowledge, and love of reading.

The four levels of *Eyewitness Readers* are aimed at different reading abilities, enabling you to choose the books that are exactly right for your children:

Level 1, for **Preschool to Grade 1**
Level 2, for **Grades 1 to 3**
Level 3, for **Grades 2 and 3**
Level 4, for **Grades 2 to 4**

The "normal" age at which a child begins to read can be anywhere from three to eight years old, so these levels are intended only as a general guideline.

No matter which level you select, you can be sure that you are helping your child learn to read, then read to learn!

A DK PUBLISHING BOOK
www.dk.com

Created by Leapfrog Press Ltd.

Project Editor Naia Bray-Moffatt
Art Editor Andrew Burgess

For DK Publishing
Senior Editor Linda Esposito
Senior Art Editor Diane Thistlethwaite
U.S. Editor Regina Kahney
Production Josie Alabaster
Picture Researcher Liz Moore
Illustrator Roger Stewart

Reading Consultant
Linda B. Gambrell, Ph.D.

First American Edition, 1999
2 4 6 8 10 9 7 5 3
Published in the United States by DK Publishing, Inc.
95 Madison Avenue, New York, New York 10016

Library of Congress Cataloging-in-Publication Data
Cottringer, Anne
Movie magic : a star is born / by Anne Cottringer. -- 1st American ed.
p.   cm. -- (Eyewitness readers. Level 3)
Summary: Follows a girl as she auditions for a part in a science fiction movie,
spends a day filming at a movie studio, meets all the people involved in the making of
a film, and attends the gala opening to see the results.
ISBN 0-7894-4009-1 (hardcover). -- ISBN 0-7894-4008-3 (pbk.)
1. Motion pictures--Production and direction Juvenile literature.
[1. Motion pictures--Production and direction.]   I. Title.
II. Series.
PN1995.9.P7C66 1999
791.43 023--dc21   98-53325
                                               CIP
                                               AC

Color reproduction by Colourscan, Singapore
Printed in Hong Kong

The publisher would like to thank the following
for their kind permission to reproduce their photographs:
Key: t=top, a=above, b=below, l=left, r=right, c=center

Andrew Burgess: 12, 44-5; Dorling Kindersley Picture Library: 6, 7br, 10tr, 10tc, 13t,
26t, 28-9t, 42-3b, 43tr, 45br/ Dave King: 2, 23tr /Evolution FX/Geoff Brightling: 34,
35tr, tc /Museum of the Moving Image: 24t /Gary Ombler: 21cr, 21br, 22b;
Garden Picture Library: 16b; Kobal Collection: 9br, 20tr;
National Motor Museum: 31tr; Planet Earth Pictures: 33t, c;
Polygram: "The Borrowers" 38; Stock Market/Richard Berenholtz: 33b

Special thanks to Angels & Bermans Fancy Dress Shop for permission
to photograph the costumes on page 12 and Tony Child Post Production
for permission to photograph his editing equipment.

Contents

EYEWITNESS ◉ READERS

Level
3
GRADES 2 and 3

MOVIE MAGIC

A STAR IS BORN

Written by Anne Cottringer

DK

DK PUBLISHING, INC.

The audition

"Please will you let me come with you?"
As Caz spoke these words she pointed to
an imaginary spaceship. She was
auditioning for a small part in a new
science fiction movie called *Starsearcher*.

The movie's casting director had come to Caz's school for the auditions. She had brought the script and the storyboard, which explained the story in pictures, shot by shot.

Caz was trying for the part of Zanuck, the hero's younger sister. In the movie, Zanuck longs to go with her older sister on a quest to save their dying planet.

Storyboards are worked out in detail.

Caz studied drama at school and loved acting. As she read the lines, she tried to speak clearly and put real feeling into every word.

Caz finished reading from the script, then smiled while the casting director took her picture and noted her height.

The movie script may be changed many times.

Caz wanted the part badly – especially when she heard that Deborah Ray, her favorite actor, was starring as the hero, Zara.

The next few days were tense for Caz as she waited to hear if she had gotten the part.

Then one morning her mother called her to the phone. It was the movie studio! Caz's hands trembled as she took the phone from her mother…she *had* gotten the part!

Her parents signed a contract and a permission form allowing her to be in the film. Caz could hardly wait to go to the studio for her day's filming.

A contract to act

Movie actors sign contracts (written agreements) with the film studio before they start filming. If the actor is a child, his or her parents must sign for them.

The big day

At last the big day arrived! Caz was so excited she woke even before the alarm clock rang. At 6.30 a.m. she was picked up by her chaperone (SHAP-uh-rone), Kirsty, who would look after her all day. They arrived at the studio gates at 7.00 a.m. for Caz's makeup call, and were given security cards.

The studio was the size of a small town. Caz and Kirsty made their way to the *Starsearcher* production office to check in. Then they walked through the busy lot to the makeup department.

Studio

Universal Studios at Orlando, Florida, is the world's largest studio complex. It even has its own police department.

In the makeup department Caz took her place in a row of people sitting in front of mirrors. They were being transformed into creatures from the planet Spartalus.

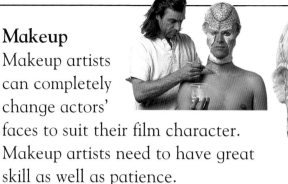

Makeup
Makeup artists can completely change actors' faces to suit their film character. Makeup artists need to have great skill as well as patience.

Caz watched in the mirror as the makeup artist glued a plastic mask over her head and hair. It felt cold.

"Don't worry," said the makeup artist. "You'll soon get used to it." Then he turned Caz's chair toward him and began to apply different colors and shades of makeup. For the final touch, he painted veins all over Caz's head.

Two hours later, Caz nearly jumped out of her skin when she looked in the mirror. A lizard-skinned alien stared back at her – Caz had been turned into Zanuck!

"Okay, Zanuck! Off we go to wardrobe!" said Kirsty.

"Do you think we might see Deborah Ray in here?" whispered Caz.

"No chance," laughed Kirsty. "The big stars have their own private dressing rooms."

Among racks of weird-looking outfits, one of the wardrobe assistants picked out a scaly lizard body skin for Caz.

"Where do you get all these amazing outfits?" asked Caz.

"We have lots of tailors who make them from a costume designer's drawings," said the assistant. "Then I fit them to people like you!"

After a few tries, they found the right size for Caz.

"Not even your parents will recognize you now," laughed Kirsty.

"Your call is in half an hour," said Kirsty. "Shall we see a set being built?"

"Wow!" cried Caz as they peered through a large sliding door marked Sound Stage B.

The stage was like a huge warehouse – except there were painters, carpenters, and plasterers everywhere.

A woman stood in the middle of the set, studying a plan and chatting with a carpenter. She was the production designer, responsible for designing the sets and overseeing their building and decoration.

Caz took a walk around the set. Suddenly she found herself in a labyrinth (lab-ER-inth). Caz remembered from the script that Zara must find her way through this maze to reach a dragon guarding a magic crystal. Zara needs the crystal to save her planet.

Lost in the labyrinth
Hedge mazes have always been popular in grand European gardens. The puzzles are usually solved within 30 minutes.

Caz decided to try the winding path-
ways of the maze herself. But it was harder
than she expected. Suddenly she found
herself at a dead end – with no way out!

"Help!" she cried. "Help!"

A friendly carpenter soon appeared
and led Caz out to a relieved Kirsty.

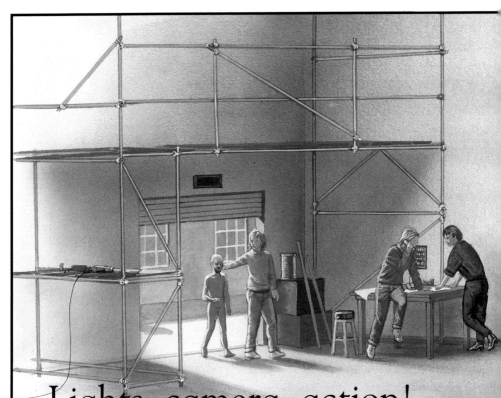

Lights, camera, action!

Kirsty took Caz to the set where Caz's first scene would be shot. Caz couldn't believe how many people there were – camera operators, lighting technicians, makeup artists, actors, and many others whom Caz couldn't identify.

Suddenly Caz felt nervous. She would have to act in front of all these people!

She began to practice her lines in her head. Then a woman came to take her onto the set. She was the assistant director, or AD for short. It was her job to make sure everyone was ready for each shot.

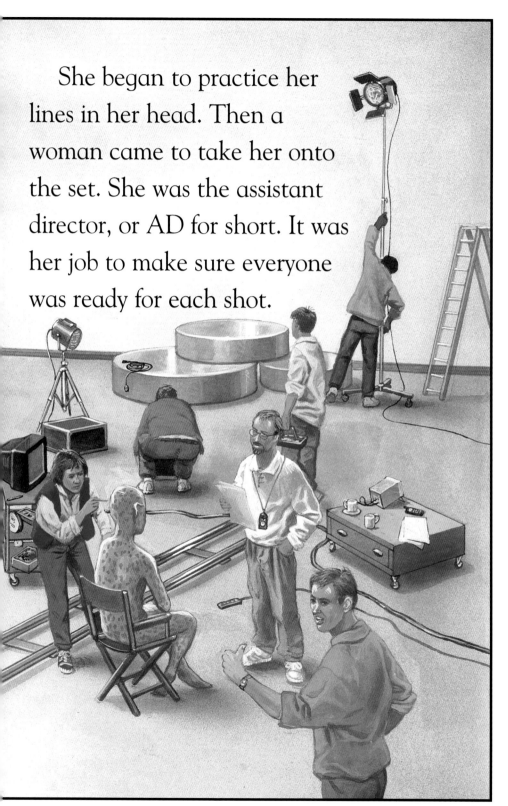

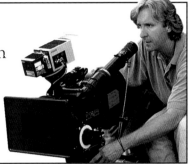

The AD introduced Caz to the director, the person in overall control of how the movie looks.

"In this scene, Caz, you are desperate to go with Zara," explained the director. "When Zara finishes her lines, I want you to rush toward her pleading 'Take me with you.' "

As Caz walked toward a taped mark on the floor which showed her where to stand, someone shouted, "Watch your backs!" Behind her came a camera on a wheeled support. It was being pushed along a set of steel tracks.

Caz jumped out of the way just in time. The next time the camera moved, it would be following her across the floor toward Zara in a tracking shot.

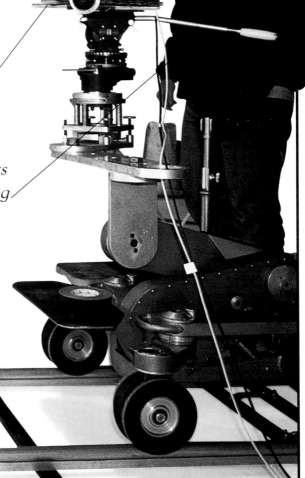

Stainless steel rods to support extra parts such as a zoom lens

Camera operator works camera during shooting

The camera can move along steel rails called a dolly track

While Caz waited on her mark, the focus puller measured the distance between the camera and Caz, then adjusted the focus ring on the camera. "Right, she's in focus now," he called to the camera operator.

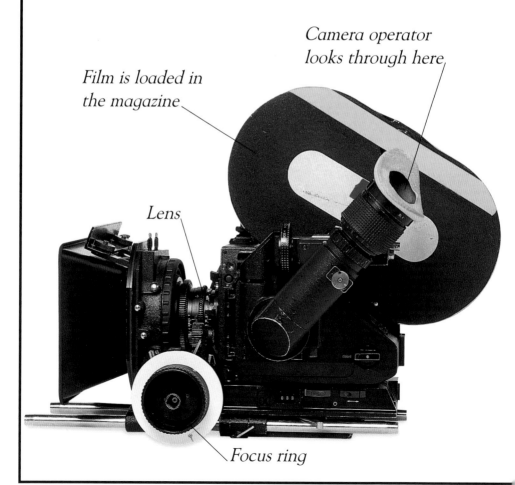

Camera operator looks through here

Film is loaded in the magazine

Lens

Focus ring

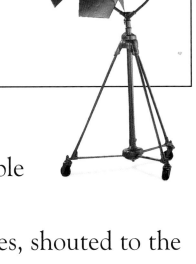

The director of photography, responsible for lighting and the choice of camera angles, shouted to the chief electrician to "flood it."

A few moments later, a soft golden light filled the set. It seemed to match Zanuck's mood of sadness and yearning.

Just as Caz was thinking how hot she felt under the glare of so many lights, someone lowered what looked to Caz like a fishing pole from above her head.

"What are you going to catch with that?" asked Caz.

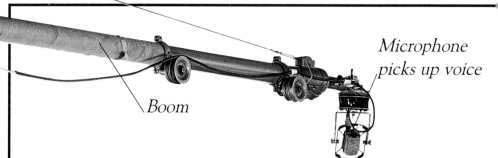

Boom

Microphone
picks up voice

"Your voice, I hope!" came the reply
from a young man holding the pole.
He had headphones on. "My job is to
keep the microphone as close to you
as I can without it being seen."

Just then Deborah Ray walked onto
the set. Caz felt her throat go dry.
She'd never be able to speak a word in
front of such a famous actor! Luckily
the director seemed to know what Caz
was thinking. He came and said some
encouraging words.

During the first run-through, Caz
stumbled over her lines. She blushed a
deep red. "Thank goodness for green
makeup," she thought to herself.

There were two more run-throughs
before the director was ready to shoot
the scene.

"Final checks!" shouted the AD.
Instantly a makeup woman was at Caz's
side, touching up her makeup. Caz felt
very important.

The clapperboard
This is filmed and "clapped" at the start of each take (a sequence of filming) so that the sound and picture can be matched up.

"Quiet, everyone!" called the AD. "Run sound!"

The sound recordist checked the microphone, then called, "Running!"

"Run camera!" ordered the AD next.

"Camera running!" replied the camera operator.

The clapper loader held up the clapperboard in front of the camera and shouted, "Slate 66, Take One!" He snapped the boards together and moved quickly away.

"Action!" called the director.

Deborah Ray began to speak her lines.

Caz was so distracted by the clack of the clapperboard, she completely forgot when she was supposed to move.

"Cut!" shouted the director.

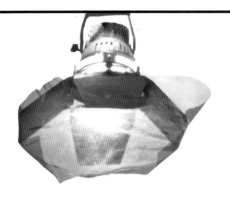

Caz jolted into action and began to move across the room.

"Cut! Cut!" called the director again. "Cut means stop!"

Caz felt the heat rise in her face. The makeup woman fussed over her again.

While the woman dabbed at her face, Caz watched an electrician put another gel on one of the lights. It made the light on the set even more golden.

Gels

Different effects can be achieved by placing these clear colored sheets over lights. They are used to create atmosphere and mood.

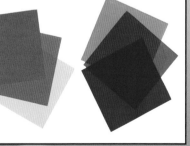

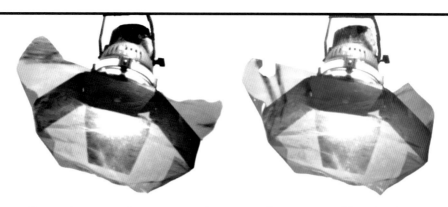

"Let's go for another take!" called the AD.

The clapper loader called out, "Slate 66, Take Two!"

This time everything went all right for Caz, but Deborah Ray forgot *her* lines. Caz feel better when she realized that even famous actors sometimes got their lines wrong. They had to do the scene six times before they got everything right and the director was happy.

"Come on. Time for lunch," said Kirsty.

Caz realized she was starving. She hadn't eaten anything since breakfast at six o'clock that morning.

Caz and Kirsty ate lunch in a large canteen. It was like being at a banquet of the bizarre, as they rubbed shoulders with aliens from Spartalus, knights from medieval times, and ladies from the last century. Caz sat next to a pirate who was in a film called *Treasure Trove*. The actor told Caz that in real life he worked as a part-time gardener.

Trailers

When shooting for weeks at a time on location (outside the studio), the actors and crew travel and live in trailers.

"Where's Deborah Ray?"asked Caz.

"The really big stars have their own room or trailers where they rest and eat," Kirsty replied.s

Special effects

After lunch Caz had a second scene where she waves goodbye to Zara, who is flying away in her spaceship. However, when she got to the set, instead of vehicles and buildings there was just a large blue wall.

"This is going to look pretty bare!" said Caz. "Is that blue wall supposed to be the sky?"

"No," smiled Kirsty. "This is where the magic comes in! That blue screen acts like a blank background for the scene. Later the director and special effects people will put in the background. Crowds of people can be added: city streets, hairy monsters – almost anything you want. We'll go and see how it works later."

This astronaut is filmed in front of a blue screen, ready to go anywhere.

Things heat up for the astronaut when this background of a volcanic landscape is added.

A night out on the town is also fun!

After they filmed the scene, Kirsty took Caz to a studio where a model maker showed them a small-scale version of Zara's spaceship flying through the sky.

"We're filming this model," explained the model maker. "Then, using a computer, we'll combine it with the scene you've just been in. We'll also add a

This light changes the color of the clouds

The model is suspended in a water tank

This light colors the bottom of the spacecraft

*Different gels create
different lighting effects*

*A high speed camera
shoots in close-up.*

larger model of the spaceport as a
background. But we need to have a blue
screen behind you for it to work."

"That's brilliant!" cried Caz.
"Could you do some movie magic so that
Zanuck goes with Zara after all?"

"Sure! We could film you in front of
the blue screen clinging on to something,
put it together with Zara's spaceship –
and you would be flying through space
hanging on to the wing of the spaceship!"

"I'm not sure I'd like to travel that
way!" laughed Caz.

Next, Kirsty took Caz to see the fierce dragon that guards the magic crystal. But the only dragon Caz could see was a sort of skeleton on a computer screen.

"It's called a wire frame," explained the woman at the computer. "We create a three-dimensional image of the dragon on the computer first and then use a software program to mold the dragon's muscles and paint in the skin."

"But how does Zara get to fight the dragon if it's on a screen?" asked Caz.

The tail can be made bigger or smaller by stretching the lines of the wire frame.

"The dragon is programmed to move, and special effects experts then combine this computer image with the scene of Zara in the maze," she said.

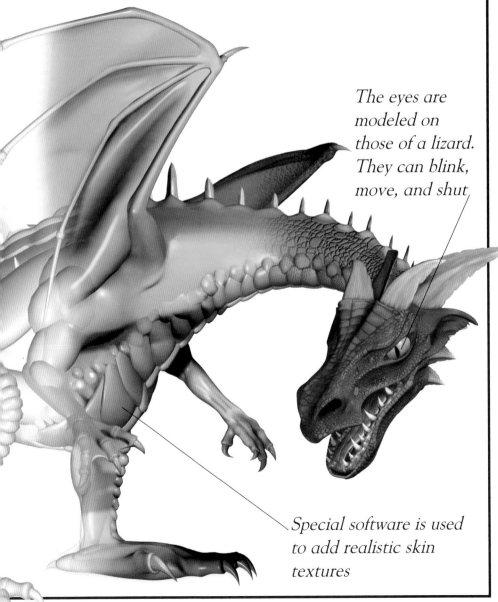

The eyes are modeled on those of a lizard. They can blink, move, and shut

Special software is used to add realistic skin textures

The final scene

Caz went back to the set for her last scene in which Zara returns to Spartalus with the magic crystal. But suddenly the AD shouted, "Where's the crystal?"

Props

Props can range from simple items such as pens to million-dollar models. These props are from the film *The Borrowers*.

It was nowhere to be seen. The props manager, in charge of all the items needed on the set, scurried around looking for it while everyone waited.

Caz decided to pay a quick visit to the bathroom. As she opened the door, something glittery caught her eye. Beside the sink sat the magic crystal.

Caz carried her treasure back to the set and handed it to Zara. Everyone on the set cheered.

"Bravo! You've saved Spartalus!"

Caz smiled and smiled.

"So that's where I left it!" cried the props manager, looking relieved. "Thanks for finding it for me."

"Places, everyone, and final checks!" shouted the AD.

For this scene the camera was mounted on a crane that held a little platform for the operator and focus puller. The crane started up high and came down so that the shot ended with a close-up of the crystal.

"Action!" called the director. Together with a group of other Spartalusians, Caz ran across the set swinging her ray gun above her head. Suddenly the ray gun flew out of her hand and whizzed toward the camera. It hit the focus puller right on the head.

"Good shot!" laughed the camera operator as he lowered the platform and returned the ray gun to Caz.

They shot the scene again, and this time Caz held on firmly to her ray gun. There were no more mishaps.

"That's it for the day!" said Kirsty. "Time to change Zanuck back into Caz."

"I've enjoyed being Zanuck!"

"I'm not surprised!" laughed Kirsty. "You discovered the maze, met the dragon, and found the magic crystal. I think Zanuck is the real hero of this movie!"

"When can we see it at the movies?" asked Caz.

"In about eight months."

"Eight months!" exclaimed Caz. "How come it takes so long?"

"There's still lots to do. The film that was shot today will be sent to the

laboratories to be developed and printed. Tomorrow they'll send a rush print for the director to look at. The movie

Film is stored on a roll in cans

has to be edited, then the sound track has to be mixed and special effects have to be created. I'll show you the cutting rooms where they are editing *Starsearcher* so you can see for yourself."

Mixing console

The sound mixer uses this console to create the sound track. Each knob controls a different sound, such as footsteps or speech. The sound mixer fixes the loudness of each sound and matches it with the picture.

In the cutting room, Caz and Kirsty found the editor sitting in front of two computer monitors. He was editing a scene that had been shot a few days earlier in which Zara tracks down a crystal but it turns out to be a false one.

"Look at Zara's face in these two takes," said the editor to Caz. "In one she looks happy and in the other she looks suspicious. If I put the first take next to a shot of the crystal it seems like she has been fooled by the crystal.

If I put the second take in, she looks like she knows there is something wrong. Which would you choose?" he asked Caz.

"She seems much smarter where she looks suspicious of the crystal. I'd choose that one!"

"Me too!" smiled the editor.

The editor cut them together.

45

Gala opening

Eight months later, Caz received a letter from the movie studio.

"It's an invitation to the opening of *Starsearcher* at the Astoria theater!" she exclaimed breathlessly.

The great night arrived in a blaze of lights and flashbulbs. Everyone was waiting to see Deborah Ray.

Caz felt very important walking up the red carpet with her parents.

Later, in the darkness of the theater, Caz sat entranced by the screen. As her first scene approached, beads of sweat broke out on her forehead. She wasn't sure she wanted to see herself. Then in a flash, Zanuck – not Caz – appeared on the screen. After all those hours of filming, her first scene was over in minutes. So much for fame and stardom!

But Caz didn't mind. She'd enjoyed acting in the film but she knew now there was something else she'd rather do – she wanted to work behind the camera in special effects.

"Then I'll be a magician," she laughed to herself. "And make movie magic."

Glossary

Audition
The sample performance given by an actor to show his or her suitability for a particular part.

Assistant director
The person who helps the director with day-to-day filming on the set.

Boom
A lightweight metal pole used to hang a microphone over the action without being in the shot.

Camera operator
The member of the camera crew who works the camera during filming.

Casting director
The person responsible for choosing the actors to appear in the movie.

Clapperboard
A hinged board filmed at the start of each take used to match up the picture with the sound.

Costume designer
The person who designs the clothes worn by actors in a movie.

Director
The person with overal responsibility for the movie's creative and technical production.

Director of photography
The person responsible for lighting and choice of camera, lens, and film.

Dolly
A wheeled support for a camera and its operator that is used for tracking shots.

Editor
The person who puts together the individual pieces of film in the best sequence.

Focus puller
The member of the camera crew in charge of focusing the camera lens.

Production designer
The person in charge of creating the design of the movie, including sets and costumes.

Props manager
The person who buys or hires the movable objects needed on the set.

Rushes
The prints of a day's filming, "rushed" back from the laboratory to be looked at by the director and editor.

Special effects
Techniques used to create scenes that cannot be achieved by normal methods.

Storyboard
A series of cartoon-like illustrations that describe the story and what the set will look like, scene by scene.

Wardrobe
The department that provides the costumes worn by the actors.